Praise for Kathleen Petrone

and the *Academy for Public Speaking*

"When I first arrived in the United States as a Vietnamese refugee, I was scarred for life with my inability then to speak English. On a long flight from Bangkok, Thailand, I remember vividly when a flight attendant with ruby-red fingernails popped a Coca-Cola can spilling a few drops on my arm. She apologized, "I'm sorry." I didn't know what to say. She repeated again, and I still sat there in complete silence… The look of pity on her face as she moved down the aisle left me with the reality of a huge language barrier. For the rest of the flight I gazed at the sea of darkness outside the window feeling lost, hopeless, and empty. With no money, no education, and no English, how would I survive in this new country?

Fast forward to two decades later… I stood on the stage of a 3,000-seat arena competing in the Semi-Finals of Toastmasters International's 2010 World Championship of Public Speaking, an annual international event with over 25,000 contestants from 110 countries. I was placed among the top 18 speakers in the world and the experience has changed my confidence forever. Later that year, professionally I was promoted to become a vice president of a Fortune 500 company with 11 billion dollars in revenue and 41,000 employees. Looking back, not only have I survived the culture shock, the financial hardship, and the language barrier, but I've also lived the American Dream!

I will be forever indebted for my success to the kindness of the American people, the Toastmasters International organization, and especially Kathleen Petrone. From the days we coached the Youth Leadership Program together to regular invitations to speak with her students at the *Academy for Public Speaking*, Kathleen has taught me the commitment of a coach, the concentration of a mentor, and the compassion of a teacher. With Kathleen's wisdom in this book, your children will learn more than just public speaking, earn more than just the needed confidence, and become well-rounded human beings.

All parents in the world, regardless of nationality, share a universal desire for their children to be happy. Kathleen's work gives your children the key to unlock their potential; confidence in communication and making a difference in the lives of others. That's the secret to happiness."

Jimmy Thai, Distinguished Toastmaster

2010 World Championship of Public Speaking, Semi-Finalist

Founder of the Leadership Foundation Academy

San Diego, California – USA * Ho Chi Minh City, Vietnam

Praise for Kathleen Petrone

and the *Academy for Public Speaking*

"I know what stage fright is. I know how it makes you feel and how it diminishes your confidence and self-worth. After graduating from college with an engineering degree I was surprised with the challenge of making a sales presentation after my first few months on my new job. My boss, Dave, put me in charge of a critical project that was the responsibility of an engineer he had recently fired. The successful implementation of this project would bring desired recognition to our group. My first major task was to make a presentation to upper management to get them to fund the project. I had a month before the presentation to learn the project.

A week before the presentation to upper management Dave asked me to make a trial presentation in his small office. On that Friday morning I stood in his office all studied-up and ready to speak. Larry, a supervisor Dave invited, walked in the office and closed the door. I felt trapped, but started my speech with the expectation of making a good impression. However, I did not finish it. I became insecure and uncertain as the piercing eyes of Dave and Larry severed my confidence. I felt alone. My confidence unraveled. I started shaking and perspiring profusely. My tenor voice became a wobbling soprano. I felt faint. My knees weakened and I had to take a seat in a nearby chair and tuck my head between my knees to regain my composure.

I was humiliated and embarrassed. My confidence was below sea level. I wished I had taken some type of public speaking training that would have prevented me from making a spectacle of myself. It was a trauma I never wanted to experience again.

Fortunately for me, Larry was a member of Toastmasters — an international communication and leadership development non-profit organization consisting of clubs around the world. They provide a learn-by-doing program where you develop skills and techniques to overcome your fear of public speaking. We had one in my office building. Larry saw my distress signal and invited me to be his guest at their next meeting. I went and joined the club, and the rest is history. After a lot of practice, I made that presentation to upper management and didn't faint. They approved the project.

I mentioned how I could have avoided my traumatic experience had I benefited from a good public speaking program early on in my life — a program like the *Academy for Public Speaking.* A program that is tailor-made for building your self-confidence early on. It is a success-proven program administered in a fun, friendly, and failsafe environment to empower children to overcome and manage their fear of public speaking.

If you want your child to become more confident, comfortable, and competent in public speaking, then allow him or her to experience the courses offered by the *Academy for Public Speaking* where each student plays a role in making this happen for one another.

I am privileged to know Kathleen Petrone and have witnessed her *Academy for Public Speaking* program in action. I've spoken to her classes, observed her students speaking, and attended a graduation. I know how passionate, dedicated, and committed she is about graduating students who have gained the confidence, skills, and belief that they can not only deliver effective speeches in public, but can also use their voices to make a difference. It is Kathleen's intention that ends up becoming the students' realities as they open the door to their own creativity and express it in a way that will enhance their lives as they move forward.

The Academy's teaching, guiding, and encouragement have created an environment of trust where the students gladly embrace their assignments without fear, knowing they will become better because of the experience.

The students benefit by Kathleen's desire to continually build upon her success by looking for ways to make improvements to her processes and practices. She continues to bring in seasoned speakers to speak to her students and allows them to learn by observing and asking questions. She also serves as a tremendous role model by being the consummate student who sharpens her own skills through study and practice.

Whether your child is looking to gain additional confidence, smooth out rough edges, stand out in the classroom, gain an advantage in a speech contest, or go after a scholarship, the *Academy for Public Speaking* is a great place to start."

Jim Tucker, Distinguished Toastmaster

Toastmasters International World Championship of Public Speaking, Three Time Finalist

Published Author & Registered Professional Engineer

Praise for Kathleen Petrone

and the *Academy for Public Speaking*

"I met Kathleen years before learning about her *Academy for Public Speaking*. Her passion for public speaking was always obvious. Then, having had the distinct pleasure of participating in Kathleen's program, I came away impressed with the program that she provides for our young people. Her *Academy for Public Speaking* provides a structured format while encouraging individuality. This may be the reason Kathleen's students were enjoying themselves so fully. I am familiar with her curriculum developed from time tested material for adults and am impressed how this material is customized to better address the age of her students.

The skills introduced will serve these children well in their world where personal spoken communication is giving way to other forms of social communication. Their confidence gained will prove invaluable in many aspects of their futures. Confidence equals growth as a person.

The hallmark of her program is the caring Kathleen exhibits for her students' development. She understands that each child has different needs and will progress accordingly. I wish that my children could have experienced Kathleen's program when they were young."

Norm Nomura, Distinguished Toastmaster & Business Consultant

Toastmasters International World Champion of Public Speaking, Two Time Semi-Finalist

Toastmasters International District 5 Speech Contest, Eight Time Finalist & Four Time Champion

Praise for Kathleen Petrone

and the *Academy for Public Speaking*

Kathleen Petrone and I first met in August 2011. From our very first meeting I could feel Mrs. Petrone's commitment to working with children in an effort to help students build confidence, poise, and competence in front of their peers and a variety of audiences. Her experience, instructional style, and strategies for classroom management were impressive. It was an easy decision to partner with her company offering public speaking classes to our oldest elementary school students in the Del Mar Union School District.

Since that time Kathleen Petrone's professionalism, communication, responsiveness, reliability, and overall program have been exemplary. Whether she personally, or one of her talented instructors, teaches the class, the feedback from both children and parents has been outstanding. We have never had one complaint about the syllabus, expectations, outcomes, or instruction for these classes. Her classes are so popular we have even added additional sections after the registration period begins to accommodate the high interest. Families have their children return to take advanced classes as well, a true sign of a great product.

We confidently offer the *Academy for Public Speaking* classes at all eight of our school sites, with half of our schools now offering advanced classes as well. For all these reasons, I highly recommend Kathleen Petrone's *Academy for Public Speaking*.

Julie Geisbauer, Director

Early Childhood/After School Programs

Del Mar Union School District

Praise for Kathleen Petrone

and the *Academy for Public Speaking*

Schools have focused on developing reading and writing skills historically. While these two are important skills to have for a child, the third one has been overlooked or neglected. Public speaking is that third and the most important skill of the three. Listening to a good speech is like listening to a good symphony. It takes a few years of hard work and guidance from an expert to achieve that command and mastery of public speaking. Public speaking skills are essential in all walks of life. Public speaking can be mastered through hard work and proper guidance.

Kathleen Petrone is an accomplished Distinguished Toastmaster and an expert in the field of public speaking. She has worked with thousands of young children to accomplish their dream of mastering this very important skill. Kathleen's insight on the subject matter is invaluable, and it will be very useful for anyone aspiring to develop or improve his or her public speaking skills. This book is an excellent composition of the necessary ingredients to develop or improve public speaking skills for beginners as well as advanced learners.

Sarraju Nadimpalli, Design Automation Engineer
North South Foundation San Diego Chapter Coordinator

Confidence is Key!

12 Amazing Ways Public Speaking Empowers Your Child

Members of the Academy VIP with

Kathleen Petrone, President & Founder

Confidence is Key!

12 Amazing Ways Public Speaking Empowers Your Child

First Edition

Cover Design – John Surge Marketing
www.aecagency.com

ISBN-10: 1499140592
ISBN 978-1499140590

This book is dedicated to Helen Blanchard, one of the first female members of Toastmasters and the first woman who served as President of Toastmasters International. I was fortunate to meet Helen when I heard her speak in 2010. After that, I joined her club, Excelsior Toastmasters. Thank you, Helen, for paving the way for females not only in Toastmasters, but also in life. You are missed, my friend!

Special thanks to Dr. Ralph C. Smedley for creating Toastmasters International. This amazing program has transformed millions of lives worldwide since its inception in 1924. Happy 90th Birthday to Toastmasters!

This book is also dedicated to my sister-in-law, Leslie Petrone. Les, I wish you were still here to celebrate this joyous occasion with me, with your warm loving eyes and huge heart, your amazing energy and enthusiasm, your radiant smile, and your cheerful laughter. You were as proud of me as my parents are, which is pretty remarkable! May I tell the world what you said? "Public speaking is one fear I'm okay with never overcoming!" Yet you were a very powerful speaker because you spoke from your soul with such great love and concern for others.

"People doubt their beliefs, but believe their doubts.

Believe in yourself, and the world will believe in you."

James L. Oleson

President of the Napoleon Hill Foundation

Contents

Embracing the power of public speaking will significantly impact and improve the quality of your child's life. Do you want to empower your child to...

Foreword by Mila Diamond   xxiii

Introduction   1

1. Overcome Fear & Anxiety   9

2. Build Self Esteem & Confidence   15

3. Increase Self Expression & Personal Happiness   17

4. Enjoy Quality Relationships   21

5. Make Friends Easily & Choose Positive Influences   25

6. Improve Behavior & Avoid Bullying   27

7. Earn Better Grades & Develop Communication Skills 35

8. Join the Speech and Debate Team   39

9. Compete in Speech Contests & Win Scholarships   45

10. Ace Interviews – Private Schools, Colleges & Jobs   55

11. Embrace Leadership & Win Elections   57

12. Experience Success & Inspire Positive Change   63

Epilogue   73

Acknowledgements   77

About the Author   81

Foreword

In early spring of 2013, I was asked to be a judge at the Optimist International Oratorical Contest. On that gorgeous Saturday morning nineteen children and teenagers, along with over 100 public speaking enthusiasts from San Diego and North County, filled the Calvary Lutheran Church in Solana Beach. The Optimist Oratorical Contest gives youngsters the chance to speak to the world. More than $150,000 in college scholarships, funded by the Optimist International Foundation, is awarded annually from this program.

Girls and boys as young as seven and as old as seventeen took the stage one after another. I was amazed by the poise, confidence, and eloquence they displayed and by the nearly TEDx (ted.com) quality of their inspirational speeches. I must say, judging these young speakers was a daunting task! Among the girls and boys, 1st and 2nd places were won by graduates of the *Academy for Public Speaking*, founded by Kathleen Petrone, Distinguished Toastmaster. This is how I first met Kathleen. She was in the audience supporting her students with a big, warm smile while videotaping their performances on her iPhone for future coaching.

The next time I saw Kathleen was a couple of weeks later. She and I squared off as rival contestants at the District 5 Western Division Level of the annual Toastmasters International Speech Contest. At that point in the competition both of us, as well as several other contestants, had won our respective Club and Area Level Contests. However, only one contestant would move on to the District Level.

I won 1st place in that contest, but Kathleen's performance was beautiful. In the true spirit of Toastmasters' rivalry,

Kathleen and I shook hands after the contest and forged our friendship. She became my supporter as I went on to win the District and was preparing to take the international stage at the 2013 World Championship of Public Speaking.

As I was designing my speech for the International, I was also speaking daily, sometimes two or even three times a day. During that time, Kathleen invited me to be a guest speaker at the *Academy for Public Speaking* to speak to her new students and graduates – children and teens, by far the most challenging and demanding audience of all. I was surprised to see that many of Kathleen's students were ESL (English as a Second Language), like me. It's a very special opportunity when I can inspire shy ESL children and encourage them to pursue public speaking. I understood and empathized with them. It took me, a shy and introverted immigrant from Russia, a number of years to become fluent in English. It was a joy to see their surprised, smiling faces when they heard my accent as I shared my story with them.

While expressing myself in English was challenging enough, I was completely knocked out of my comfort zone by my mentor. He suggested that I speak publicly to launch my consulting career in Fortune 500 and 1000 markets. As scary as it was, I was eager to succeed so I followed my mentor's advice. I soon secured a column in a technology trade magazine and started booking speaking engagements in New York City and Chicago. As if by magic, public speaking opened doors for me, positioned me as a subject matter expert, and eventually led to my breaking the "glass ceiling" and becoming the highest paid IT (Information Technology) management consultant at a Fortune 500 company.

A few weeks after my first visit to Kathleen's *Academy for Public Speaking*, the day before I flew to Cincinnati for the International Speech Contest, Kathleen invited me to speak at a graduation ceremony for her students who had just completed one of her courses. The transformation her students had made in the short few weeks was simply phenomenal! With growing confidence, they spoke from the stage in front of the audience. I marveled at Kathleen's talent to connect with her young students and gently guide them to find their voices and express themselves fearlessly, eloquently, and with conviction. But perhaps the most precious was their sense of accomplishment! Under her skillful coaching, these children and teens have conquered one of the biggest fears that so many people share – a fear of public speaking.

A couple of days later, Kathleen joined me at the Toastmasters International Convention, where 89 contestants from 82 countries assembled to compete for the coveted title of World Champion of Public Speaking. I was getting ready to speak in front of the international audience of 2,500 people. Excitement was at its peak. Nerves were strung high. And the skill of staying cool under pressure was put to the test. Kathleen acted as my personal stylist and speaking coach, listening to my speech over and over again, giving me final suggestions in the hours leading up to the contest. Once a rival just a few months ago, Kathleen became a dear friend who inspired, supported, and cheered me on.

I was overjoyed when Kathleen called yesterday and said that she just finished writing this book. Communication is perhaps the single most important skill we can encourage in our children to help them succeed. Public speaking allows children to gain confidence and opens doors in business and in life. Kathleen Petrone, DTM, is a master public speaking coach. Her wisdom and experience in teaching children, her talent to connect, and the success stories of her students in this book will surely touch your heart and inspire you to consider teaching your child public speaking. Perhaps one day, your child will inspire change from a TED stage (ted.com) and become a role model for his or her contemporaries and generations to come.

Mila Diamond, ACB, CL

District 5 Champion of Public Speaking 2013, Toastmasters International

Keynote Inspirational Speaker, Executive and Life Success Coach at Diamond Mind International - inspiring greatness and creating enlightened leaders

San Diego, CA

Introduction

Public Speaking - From Painful to Powerful

We are not born afraid to speak. We cry and freely express our emotions as we enter this world. As infants we watch, listen, and interact to learn what words mean. When we finally speak our first word, it is extremely powerful - a cause for celebration! Our parents smile and cry as they are moved to tears by this amazing milestone.

Words can be wonderful. We use words to express our love, gratitude, compassion, and concern. Yet words can also be used as weapons. The power of the spoken word can be precious and priceless or piercingly painful.

Public speaking is the number one fear for many adults. But it is not actually the act of speaking words that most people fear. It is the reaction that may result. It is the fear of humiliation or rejection.

As a child I was a happy, outgoing, and expressive little girl. I was comfortable with who I was and extremely confident. But then one day in third grade, I received devastating news. It was my greatest childhood fear. I found out I had failed the eye exam. I would have to wear glasses.

It wasn't that I actually feared wearing glasses. I feared the reaction that might result from wearing glasses. I feared humiliation and rejection. I feared being made fun of and called names such as four eyes. I was even afraid my best friend wouldn't like me anymore because I decided I was no longer a "cool" kid.

My self-esteem was shattered. I became so uncomfortable with myself I did not want to speak. I was afraid to speak because of what might happen next. I didn't want to draw any unnecessary attention to myself for fear of being made fun of by my classmates. I wouldn't even make eye contact with my teachers. I was a smart kid who almost always knew the answers teachers wanted, but that didn't matter.

If a teacher called on me, then everyone would look at me and that would be so embarrassing!

The reality is I let my fear stop me and control my life. But why did I do that? I was the only one who decided I was unworthy. I don't actually recall anyone ever making fun of me, and my best friend didn't disown me. What I did develop from this fear of judgment were some negative behavior patterns such as not expressing myself verbally, being indecisive, and being unassertive. These bad habits negatively affected my personal relationships, and they limited my professional life.

Despite my fear and negative habits, I became a happy and successful adult. I graduated from college, became a classroom teacher, and owned a nice car and home. I was close with my family and friends. Yet my life wasn't the best it could be. When I met the man I wanted to marry, I knew I would have to take a risk and learn to express myself verbally and emotionally. I decided to confront my fear, take control, and make a change. I decided to develop my confidence, assertiveness, public speaking, and leadership skills. Though I was terrified, I joined Toastmasters. This was another major turning point in my life. Although I didn't know it at the time, I was also acquiring the skills I would need to become a successful entrepreneur a few years later once I discovered my passion and purpose in life.

I have always been passionate about teaching children, but I frequently question what, why, and how we teach children in our public school system and how much time we spend on assessment. Cursive and penmanship? Memorization and regurgitation? Multiple guess tests? We often omit essential skills such as communication, financial literacy, and applying knowledge to solve problems. Can you imagine how different, and significantly better, our nation and world would be if everyone was schooled in communication skills, financial literacy, and solving problems? Thankfully, the Common Core Standards are beginning to address our severely outdated education system.

Being comfortable with who I am and expressing myself has not only freed me from fear, but it has also given me a special gift I now excitedly share with children and adults who may be holding back and limiting themselves in life due to a lack of confidence. No matter which goals a person decides to pursue, having confidence and effective communication skills will help him or her achieve those goals and live a happier, more successful life.

In 2010, I founded the *Academy for Public Speaking* to help children become confident, effective communicators. We offer fun, interactive courses and personal coaching sessions to help children from second grade through high school (and adults) creatively express themselves as they develop confidence, public speaking, and leadership skills. Contrary to many public school systems, our program focuses on learning by doing, actually applying concepts and skills, and experimenting with new techniques rather than just constantly assessing students with tests, tests, and more tests. Through performance-based education, our students learn to provide written and verbal evaluations for their peers in a positive, helpful, and friendly manner.

Students receive an abundance of immediate feedback from their peers and teachers, including both compliments and suggestions for improvement. Academy students also learn the importance of respect, compassion, and cooperation. One of the most important lessons our students learn is their participation, opinions, and advice are essential components of the education process.

In our first three years, the *Academy for Public Speaking* empowered over 700 students to become confident, effective communicators and leaders who use their voices to inspire others and improve our world. Our graduates have also reported numerous personal benefits from our courses such as improved listening, speaking, and writing abilities, feeling more confident, giving more powerful presentations, and earning better grades in school.

Graduates of the *Academy for Public Speaking* have not only improved their relationships with themselves, their friends, and their parents, but they are also less likely to be bullied. Our graduates have experienced the empowering feeling of being in control of their fear, speaking before classmates, leading a meeting, and presenting their final speech projects to a large audience, including parents, teachers, and peers. Children who can confidently and creatively express themselves are happier, and they have an advantage in school and life. Give your child the gift that lasts a lifetime – the gift of confidence!

"I learned that courage was not the absence of fear, but the triumph over it. The brave man is not he who does not feel afraid, but he who conquers that fear."

Nelson Mandela

Former President of South Africa

Benefit #1 – Overcome Fear & Anxiety

Little Tricia* (name changed to protect privacy) sat frozen in her seat with a deer in the headlights look on her face. I had just introduced Tricia to share her first speech before a small group of her classmates. Tricia was a sweet, quiet, and very well behaved fourth grade student. I could tell Tricia didn't feel comfortable sitting there in defiance of my expectation for her to go to the front of the room and share her speech. The notes on the table indicated Tricia was prepared, but she was not ready to risk speaking. Tricia didn't move except for shaking her head slightly, slowly back and forth. Her sad, scared eyes sincerely said it all. "No, I'm sorry. I can't speak right now."

This had never happened before so I wasn't sure what to do. Then remembering my own childhood experience of how I couldn't stand to have everyone looking at me, an idea suddenly came to me. I said, "How about if we all look away and you share your speech from your seat?" Tricia nodded so I quickly said, "Okay, everybody look away," and I promptly modeled looking at the ceiling. The other students had fun following my lead. Everyone looked at the ceiling, floor, or walls or through one of the windows while Tricia sat in her seat and shared her speech. At the end of Tricia's speech, we all applauded. I felt so proud of Tricia and myself for thinking of an idea that worked.

At the end of class, Tricia approached me and asked what I wanted her to do for the following week. I had not planned to have Tricia present a speech during the next class, but then another idea came to me. "Tricia, how about sharing that same speech from the front of the classroom next week?" She smiled at me and said okay.

The following week Tricia shared her speech from the front of the classroom. After first trusting me and then herself enough to overcome her initial fear, Tricia began to embrace the power of public speaking. The formerly super shy and seriously scared girl blossomed beautifully before my eyes. First, Tricia became comfortable and confident as she confronted and conquered her fear. Then Tricia showed excitement and enthusiasm as she continued to excel with the rest of her assignments. Tricia transformed from a super shy student to a highly successful speaker in just a few weeks!

Although it is not usually this extreme, the majority of our students begin the level one course feeling some degree of nervousness, fear, or anxiety. This emotion ranges from mild nervous butterflies to extreme anxiety. During the first class we help children realize when faced with the fear of public speaking they have two choices. They can either face their fear and overcome it, or they can go through their entire lives living in fear, lacking confidence, and avoiding uncomfortable situations.

In his national bestselling book *The Success Principles*, Jack Canfield, cocreator of the *Chicken Soup for the Soul* series, refers to this as being willing to go through the "awkward stage." When we learn how to do something new, we're usually not very good at it at first. Whether you are learning how to play a sport, speak a foreign language, or play an instrument, it takes practice to become proficient.

I love T. Harv Eker's quote, "Every master was once a disaster." When it comes to public speaking, most of us are initially disasters. I certainly was. However, anyone can improve significantly in a short period of time by taking classes to practice and learn new skills. I knew my first few speeches were going to be awful and awkward, but I also knew the alternative if I didn't face my fear would be to feel awkward about it forever.

Fortunately, children are wise and they are more willing to make a change than adults. Children quickly realize their choices are to either step outside their comfort zones for a few weeks to grow and make changes for the better or they can spend their entire lifetimes living in fear. Just think of how many adults you know who fear public speaking. As adults, we tend to become set in our ways and are unwilling to change. You can help your child avoid the pain of growing up feeling uncomfortable, dreading public speaking, and missing out on opportunities in life because of it.

The trouble with avoidance and living in fear is it limits your opportunities in life. If you are afraid to speak in front of others, how will you achieve your goals and dreams? Fortunately, children are more open to change. Once they decide to confront and overcome the fear of public speaking, they rapidly gain more confidence and improve their communication skills.

"My son overcame a stutter that had rendered him speechless, but he was left with a low level of confidence when speaking in front of a group. He took the level one course at the Academy for Public Speaking two years ago. He enjoyed it so much that he took the level one course again and then the advanced course. He is now so confident speaking in front of crowds, he enters oratorical competitions for fun and someday wants to be a Toastmaster just like his mentor, Kathleen Petrone."

Judith Blue, Parent of a 6th grade student, Del Mar Union School District

"Whether you think you can, or you think you can't, you're right."

Henry Ford

Founder of the Ford Motor Company

Benefit #2 - Build Self Esteem & Confidence

One of our sixth grade students, Cassandra*, was thirty seconds into her first speech, when she began crying and ran out of the room. Cassandra was so scared to come back and give her speech she decided to skip the next class. However, with some extra support Cassandra overcame her fear and presented her first project from her seat. For her next project, Cassandra spoke from the front of the room. During her graduation ceremony, Cassandra's instructor and I proudly watched as Cassandra confidently shared her persuasive charity speech in front of a large group of her classmates and their parents.

When we step outside our comfort zones, face our fears, and do something we have never done before, we gain confidence and feel proud of ourselves. At the *Academy for Public Speaking* we empower our students to become confident, effective communicators. We provide a safe, supportive, and extremely positive learning environment. One of the most valuable lessons our students learn is their participation, opinions, and advice are essential components of the education process. The goal of our courses is to help children learn to confidently, effectively, and creatively express themselves so they develop the communication and leadership skills they need to achieve their goals and dreams.

"Kathleen takes a genuine interest in her students and seeks to help them develop not only directly through her class, but also through other public speaking opportunities in the greater San Diego area.

Since my daughter began taking classes through the *Academy for Public Speaking*, other adults have commented to me how mature, engaging, and comfortable in adult conversation she is. Her confidence has grown noticeably."

Zach Hornby, Parent of a 7th grade student in the San Dieguito Union High School District

Benefit #3 - Increase Self Expression

& Personal Happiness

One of the most rewarding benefits of teaching children confidence is the ability to change a child's life. During one of our after school enrichment courses, a second grade student named Adam* refused to come to the first class. Since Adam's parents knew our courses could help him overcome his fear, Adam was reluctantly escorted into the second class by the school's childcare supervisor. Adam looked mortified and was visibly upset. The supervisor sat with Adam in the back of the classroom to give him time to calm down and observe the environment. Adam just watched us that day.

At the beginning of the third class, I saw Adam standing outside the door peeking in through the window. I invited Adam in and he sat next to me. As the course progressed,

Adam intently observed all that was occurring. He always felt safest in the seat next to me and although Adam didn't speak much during his first course, he learned a lot. Even though Adam had what would be considered a slow start for most students, it was exactly what he needed to overcome his intense fear. Now Adam has participated in our level one course twice, and he has also completed the advanced course.

I remember how rewarding it felt when Adam finally found the desire and courage to speak. As Adam shared his first speech from the front of the room, it warmed my heart to see how patient, supportive, and proud his classmates could be.

If you have a fear of public speaking, think back to your childhood. What was your turning point? When did you become afraid of what might happen when you speak and why? Are fear and anxiety negatively affecting and limiting your happiness and success?

What about your child? Is your child afraid to speak during class or in front of a group of peers or adults? What are your child's dreams? Does your child have the confidence and communication skills to do whatever his or her heart desires? Do you wish your child seemed happier or more confident? Set your child up for success. The *Academy for Public Speaking* transforms public speaking from painful to powerful and gives children the gift that will last a lifetime – the gift of confidence!

"We deeply appreciate that Kathleen has designed such wonderful courses for young children. In the classes students not only get a chance to practice speech skills, but they also learn to research and organize well for each topic. Step by step through the class, I have seen my child build her confidence on the stage, from shy to willing to try, and then happy to share her opinions with others while making eye contact from the stage.

All of my family members are really happy to see my daughter's growth from these amazing classes and teachers. We really feel lucky that my child has joined these classes. I deeply believe this is an essential element in the education of this new century. Thank you, Kathleen."

Meiling Yueh, Parent of a 3rd grade student in the Del Mar Union School District

Benefit #4 - Enjoy Quality Relationships

Tricia*, a formerly super shy fourth grade student, improved tremendously throughout her level one course. The final speech project for the level one course is a persuasive charity speech. Since Tricia's mother runs a non-profit organization, Tricia chose to represent her mother's charity. During rehearsal Tricia's classmates and I heard her speech for the first time. We thought it was really sweet Tricia chose to represent her mother's charity, but then Tricia's speech became emotional in a way we had not expected. Tricia shared, "My mom spends so much time on her charity helping other children. I am jealous, and I wish she would pay more attention to me."

We were shocked, yet amazed at Tricia's sincerity. What impressed me most though was the metamorphosis from this extremely shy girl who had been afraid to get out of her seat and speak during her first speech to the clearly confident girl who now, just six weeks later, stood before us freely expressing an emotion she formerly suppressed.

Although we teach public speaking and leadership skills at the *Academy for Public Speaking*, the most essential skill our students learn is to be more confident. The quality of your relationships begins with you and your relationship with yourself. If you are happy with yourself and like who you are, then other people will be more inclined to like you.

We enjoy being with people who are confident because they tend to be happier and more fun to be around. Since insecure people are nervous, it can feel awkward to interact with them. During her second class when Tricia was so nervous she refused to get up and give her speech her classmates were uncertain about what to say and how to act. The children looked at me curiously to see how I was going to react because they weren't sure how to respond to this situation.

I remembered how uncomfortable I felt as a child when everyone looked at me, and I wanted to eliminate the awkward tension. Being silly and having a little fun seemed like the perfect solution. Tricia agreed to share her speech if we all looked at someone or something else besides her. I stared at the ceiling so the children could clearly see I was not looking at Tricia. The students happily followed my lead. Everyone looked at the ceiling, floor, or walls or through one of the windows. Although we felt silly, our actions helped eased the tension and made the experience really special. Most importantly, Tricia felt supported.

After her second class as Tricia became a more confident speaker, she relaxed and started having fun while she shared her speeches. Tricia's improved level of confidence put her audience at ease and then they relaxed and enjoyed her speeches too.

The rewards for teaching children to be confident, effective communicators are immense. As a child I was so insecure I wouldn't even look at my teachers because I didn't want them to call on me. Later in life as a classroom teacher, I realized how much more interesting a class is for everyone when more people are actively engaged and participating. I take pride in knowing the *Academy for Public Speaking* encourages students to have the courage and confidence to speak up and participate in class. Everyone benefits when more people express their thoughts and exchange ideas.

When I founded the *Academy for Public Speaking*, I didn't realize how much our program would help students improve their relationships with their parents. To know Tricia became confident enough to express her feelings of jealousy to her mother really touched my heart. Having the communication skills and confidence to effectively express your emotions, needs, and desires is essential for maintaining happy, successful relationships.

Benefit #5 - Make Friends Easily

& Choose Positive Influences

As a child, I don't recall how I made friends. It seemed to come naturally for me. But, unfortunately, making friends doesn't come naturally for every child.

At the *Academy for Public Speaking* we offer personal coaching sessions for children and adults for a variety of reasons. Personal coaching topics include improving communication skills, increasing confidence, expressing thoughts, and making friends. Additional areas of focus include preparing for school projects, professional presentations, speech contests, and interviews.

While coaching a student who was having difficulty making friends, I realized the challenge was not that he didn't understand how to make friends, but he lacked confidence. His lack of confidence made his social interactions feel awkward to him. If his interactions felt awkward to him, then they probably felt awkward to the people he wanted to have as friends.

Increasing your child's level of confidence will make it easier for him or her to make friends. As a parent, you are probably extremely concerned that your child chooses the "right" friends and does not get involved with the "wrong" crowd. Children who are confident are more likely to make wise choices when it comes to choosing good friends and avoiding people who are bad influences.

Benefit #6 - Improve Behavior & Avoid Bullying

The students who attended the first session of the *Academy for Public Speaking* classes will always hold a special place in my heart as the original group of *Academy for Public Speaking* students. Therefore, I was quite surprised when I recently learned one of my original and best students, who is now a sophomore in high school, shared he was frequently not very well behaved when he was in elementary school. I met Hanrui during his seventh grade year, and I was immediately impressed by how polite and respectful he was. Hanrui not only listened and participated in class, but he also excelled. Hanrui eagerly embraced the lessons and immediately applied all of the concepts he was learning. It was such a pleasure being his teacher!

To my delight, Hanrui and his friends continued taking the entire series of classes in succession. Early on during his first course, I could tell this bright and talented young student had enormous potential. I encouraged Hanrui to apply his new knowledge and skills outside of class by competing in speech contests. Just two months after Hanrui began taking classes he entered his first speech contest. I beamed with pride as he competed and won, competed and won, competed and won. I think I was just as proud of Hanrui as his parents were! Hanrui has continued to compete in and win speech contests every year since I met him. I always look forward to the annual speech contests because I enjoy seeing the graduates and how much they have grown not only as speakers, but also as individuals.

In 2013, we began offering a free one hour introduction to public speaking class for prospective students to learn more about the *Academy for Public Speaking* and how becoming a confident, effective communicator can positively impact their lives. As part of the class, I always invite a few graduates to be special guest speakers. The graduates share how they initially felt about public speaking, what they liked about the classes, what they learned, and how our courses have helped them. Each graduate also shares a speech on a topic of his or her choice. I was honored and amazed when Hanrui shared the following story while he was a special guest speaker for an introduction class full of prospective students.

"This year in English class my teacher gave us a book to read called *The Metamorphosis* by Franz Kafka. *The Metamorphosis* is about a man named Gregor Samsa, a traveling salesman who wakes up one morning and finds out he's become a cockroach. Throughout the entire story Gregor struggles to adapt to his new appearance not only with his family, but also with his co-workers and manager. At the end of the story Gregor finds himself realizing the type of person he is and how his appearance affects his status greatly.

After we read this book, my teacher gave us a prompt, which was "What was your metamorphosis?" When I was in elementary school, I attended three different schools, which meant my teachers and peers were new to me every two or three years. In elementary school I would talk back to the teachers. I would always be mean and be a bully toward those I didn't feel were worthy enough to talk to me. In third grade, my teacher had to send my parents weekly behavioral notices just to tell them how well or how badly I'd been behaving in class. In second and third grade I had to move my behavior clip from good green to warning yellow and sometimes even call home red. All the way up to sixth grade I was like that.

In sixth grade at the very end of the year, we had to write a speech. Every single student had to write a speech for promotion. From each class there would be one person who would represent the class at promotion. After I'd written my speech and I was going up to present it, I couldn't even read my note cards since I was so nervous. After I had given my speech, my teacher looked around at the class and said, "Some of you did a very nice job, but some of you looked like you were standing up there with a gun pointed to your head, like an interrogation," and she looked right at me.

That summer my mom discovered a place called the *Academy for Public Speaking*, and she enrolled me. At first I didn't know what to expect. After walking into the conference room for the first class and seeing people I knew and people I would know for the rest of my life, I realized this place was really a place for me to grow with my peers and for myself as well.

The *Academy for Public Speaking* has taught me to appreciate communication on an oral level and also on a material level as well. From playing in my school orchestra with my cello, the communication I experience can be enjoyed non-verbally. By writing for my school newspaper and with the skills I have learned at the *Academy for Public Speaking* on how to be concise and to the point, I write better articles and submit better papers for my English class and my school newspaper.

As a member of the speech and debate team and an avid competitor at speech contests held outside of school, I have realized while standing up there with a suit and tie on in front of a group of strangers my words and what I am able to communicate to them can have a profound impact on a group of people I didn't even know.

At the end of the day from sixth grade all the way till now, I have grown through my ability to speak. I have grown through my training at the *Academy for Public Speaking*, and I have grown through my appreciation for communication on different levels and in different types of communication. That is why my metamorphosis could only have occurred through sixth grade, through elementary school, through behavioral changes, and most importantly through the *Academy for Public Speaking*."

Wow! To know I've had this kind of an impact makes me feel very proud and extremely grateful that I have discovered and am living my purpose in life. You never know whose life you will touch or what type of impact you will make. I was truly surprised to learn about Hanrui's past behavior. I have always seen him as a model student who embraces opportunities, volunteers his time, and inspires others with his positive messages. I am honored to know I have played a significant role in helping Hanrui transform his outlook, actions, and life to become the highly successful person he is today.

I know the bullying issue all too well. There was a really mean girl in high school who was one year older. She would always try to taunt me. I didn't understand why at the time, but now I realize she felt insecure about herself, and her issues really had nothing to do with me. However, that didn't make the bullying any less traumatic. My solutions were to avoid and ignore her. Fortunately, those ideas worked pretty well when I was in high school.

As a teacher, I was challenged with bullying issues involving my students. Despite their insecurities, bullies are wise. They only bully others when they think no one is watching. Other than constant surveillance, what can we do to solve the problem of bullying?

We can teach our children to be confident. Confident children are not only less likely to be targeted by bullies, but they are also often willing to speak up and call bullies on their inappropriate behavior. Furthermore, teaching children to be confident eliminates their insecurities and the need to bully others to feel better about themselves.

Benefit #7 - Earn Better Grades

& Develop Communication Skills

At the *Academy for Public Speaking* students learn a simple organizational structure they can apply whether they are writing a paragraph, planning an essay or a speech, or delivering an impromptu speech. Students learn how to organize their thoughts in a logical, concise, and interesting manner. Children who can organize their thoughts well verbally and in writing earn higher grades and perform better in school. Our graduates have reported receiving better grades and doing exceptionally well on projects that involve presentations. It is not uncommon for our students to excitedly share they have received perfect scores on projects and assignments.

At the *Academy for Public Speaking* we focus on students learning and applying new concepts and skills. Through performance-based education, our students are actively engaged throughout each class session, and they receive an abundance of opportunities and immediate feedback from their instructor and peers. The small, supportive, and extremely positive environment allows students to feel safe stepping outside their comfort zones, experimenting with new presentation techniques, and stepping into their power as leaders.

Our students are positive, supportive, helpful, and friendly. They listen to one another and they learn the importance of teamwork, cooperation, and respect. However, our students also learn the artful skill of providing suggestions for improvement to their classmates in an encouraging manner so their comments will be well received. The students also share compliments during their written and verbal evaluations to acknowledge their classmates for improving their communication and presentation skills.

Students whose first language is not English also benefit tremendously from being in such an intensive, language rich environment. Enrique* began his level one class feeling extremely shy and inhibited since he did not understand or speak very much English. However, in this ideal environment, Enrique quickly began to flourish. As he continually received positive feedback and support from his classmates and me, Enrique began to gain confidence. He smiled, he laughed, and he learned. I suspect Enrique learned much more than what was written in the lesson plans. I suspect Enrique learned priceless, valuable lessons he will remember for the rest of his life.

"Success is all about attitude, knowledge, and the willingness to learn and grow."

T. Harv Eker

Founder of *Peak Potentials Training*

Motivational Speaker

Author of the #1 Bestseller *Secrets of the Millionaire Mind*

Benefit #8 - Join the Speech and Debate Team

"I came to the *Academy for Public Speaking* after I joined and then immediately quit my speech and debate club. Going into the speech and debate club, I thought I would learn how to speak in front of many people. Instead I learned that I'd have to go into a speech and debate competition without any instruction on how to do it."

Neil Majumdar, 9th grade, Poway

The sad reality is Neil was not only ready and willing to learn public speaking skills, but he also had the desire. Unfortunately, Neil's school had nothing to offer him. Fortunately, Neil's parents discovered the *Academy for Public Speaking* and enrolled him in our level one course.

It's a shame public speaking skills are not taught in our schools. Public speaking is such an essential skill for achieving success and happiness, both personally and professionally. I successfully avoided the experience of taking a public speaking course until I was in college. Then I knew I had to take the course if I wanted to earn my degree.

I felt terrified and rightfully so. I had never received any instruction regarding public speaking. Therefore, I was absolutely terrible and it was a terribly traumatic experience. It was so traumatic, in fact, I wanted nothing more to do with public speaking for the next 15 years! Even though I felt reluctant to finally face this fear, I realized not confronting and overcoming this fear was costing me. It was costing me a lot. My fear was holding me back and limiting my options in life. It was time to make the transformation from painful to powerful.

It amazes me despite the decades that have passed since my childhood, we still do not teach communication skills, such as public speaking, to our children while they are in school. If children learned this essential skill in school, then they would become comfortable speaking and giving presentations. Teaching public speaking techniques in school can prevent children from growing up and experiencing the intense fear so many adults feel. Although avoidance is a common coping mechanism, it is certainly not an ideal solution.

Some schools now require students to give presentations. However, just as Neil's example of joining his speech and debate team shows, schools also generally fail to provide any accompanying instruction regarding how students can deliver effective presentations. Certainly forcing students to just get up there and do it is counterproductive and not in their best interest. Even worse, many teachers make the mistake of requiring rote memorization. However, this is not speaking. This is recitation!

The time we waste having students memorize and recite words in a precise order could be better spent having them use their brain power to actually think, analyze, apply, discuss, debate, solve, etc. Joining a speech and debate team is a superb way for students to not only build their confidence, but also develop and enhance their thinking, problem solving, and communication skills.

After recently emailing a graduate from our masters course to wish her a happy birthday, Irene wrote the following reply. "Hi! I haven't seen you in such a long time! Thanks so much! You know what's funny? I'm currently at a debate tournament!!! I'm doing great thanks to your help. I've learned to be more confident, assertive, and hold my ground." Sincerely, Irene

Taking classes at the *Academy for Public Speaking* is not only an excellent way to inspire students to join their schools' speech and debate teams, but also to prepare them to be successful when they do.

"Before enrolling in the Academy for Public Speaking, my son, Austin, never really considered public speaking, and neither did I. Now, after completing Mrs. Petrone's courses, Austin is not only a successful public speaker, who speaks at numerous events, but he is also a captain on his school's speech and debate team. The Academy for Public Speaking has really opened up a whole new world for my son."

Andrea Sun, Parent of a 10th grade student, San Dieguito Union High School District

Although Neil initially felt nervous about public speaking, he knew mastering this essential skill and increasing his level of confidence would empower him and enrich the quality of his life. After Neil completed his level one course, he immediately enrolled in our advanced course to continue developing his public speaking skills.

"Having gone through these classes, I now feel much more confident going into a speech and debate club where I can participate in these competitions and have a chance of winning. I plan to join my school's speech and debate team next year now that I feel confident and adequately prepared."

Neil Majumdar, 9th grade, Poway

Benefit # 9 - Compete in Speech Contests

& Win Scholarships

Competing in speech contests is one of the best ways for your child to improve his or her skills as a public speaker. *Academy for Public Speaking* graduates have competed in contests and won top honors, cash prizes, and scholarships totaling over $12,000 since they began competing in 2011! Our graduates compete in annual speech contests held by the Optimist Club, the Lions Club, the San Diego County Fair Board, and the North South Foundation.

Each year Academy graduates win thousands of dollars in prize money, gain even more confidence, and improve their speaking skills. Because so many of the same graduates choose to take advantage of every opportunity to compete, the contests are fun *Academy for Public Speaking* reunions. I love seeing and supporting my former students at the contests!

The first group of *Academy for Public Speaking* students graduated from their level one course at the end of March in 2011. Just one week later graduates Hanrui Zhang, Austin Zhang, and Kevin Wang won 1st, 2nd, and 3rd place, respectively, in the Del Mar Solana Beach Optimist Club Oratorical Contest. Next, Hanrui competed at the second level, where he won 1st place again. Then Hanrui advanced to the final level of the competition, where he won 3rd place at the San Diego District Contest. This all happened within a few months of beginning his first course with the *Academy for Public Speaking*!

"When I first began to take public speaking lessons at the *Academy for Public Speaking*, I had little to no intention of expanding my skills to contests and competitions, as these were still vague and unexplored areas of the world of public speaking as a whole. Through encouragement from Kathleen, as well as her enthusiasm and confidence in her material she taught me, I finally took a step forward and began to enter speech contests.

Preparing for speech contests was something I had not had any experience in doing beforehand. Typing up a speech used to take months of work. Next came presentation practice. There has always been a saying circulating around that to prepare for speeches the best way to do so was to practice in front of a mirror. The first time I practiced for a contest and did that, I could not stop laughing at how unfamiliar the entire process was. Seeing the way my face changed at different times and hearing my voice echo through the room surprised me as I had never really spoken so formally.

The thing is, as I began to enter more and more contests, speaking "formally" became speaking "normally" for me. My daily conversation with peers, students, parents, and family members became easier to understand, free of filler words and hesitation. Competitive speaking really spurred a drive in me to be even better at public speaking, and they are evenly responsible for what really changed speaking from formality to normality for me."

Hanrui Zhang, 10th grade, Carmel Valley

"My son is a graduate from the *Academy for Public Speaking*. Kathleen has coached him for many different speech contests since 2011, leading to several wins, many good lessons learned, and a $2,500 scholarship. My son is a very confident public speaker now. It is also a great learning experience for the whole family. Skills learned from the *Academy for Public Speaking* are lifetime benefits."

Yu Sun, Parent of a 10th grade student, San Dieguito Union High School District

I remember when I first joined Toastmasters. I had only been a member for a few months when my friend Johnny encouraged me to compete. Johnny excitedly said, "Hey Kathleen, are you going to compete in the speech contest this year?" This idea had never occurred to me before, and honestly it sounded quite repulsive. I looked at Johnny like he was crazy, and I let the excuses fly. They rolled right off my tongue without any hesitation. "That sounds like a lot of work. I don't have enough time. I don't have a good topic."

Then Johnny did something very juvenile. After hearing all of my very common excuses, Johnny looked me right in the eye and with a mischievous grin he accusingly inquired, "Kathleen, are you chicken?" It may have been a juvenile tactic, but it was effective... even though I was an adult! I realized Johnny was right. I was making excuses since competing in a speech contest was outside my comfort zone.

It was like riding on a rollercoaster for the first time. I was so scared to do it at first, but as soon as I did it once I loved the thrill of it! Now I take advantage of every opportunity to compete, and I encourage my students to do the same. The majority of them have never considered competing in speech contests either, but many of my students choose to step outside their comfort zones and accept the challenge.

My friend and mentor, Jim Tucker, who is a Distinguished Toastmaster and a three time finalist at the Toastmasters World Championship of Public Speaking, presented a seminar called "Lose to Win" during which he talked about the value of competing. Jim shared a quote I really love, "There is no comfort in the growth zone and no growth in the comfort zone." (unknown author) The rewards for stepping outside your comfort zone and encouraging others to do so are absolutely amazing!

Your child will improve his or her skills tremendously by observing other speakers who are striving to be the very best they can be. The Lions Club Student Speakers Contest is a highly competitive annual speech contest for students in 9th-12th grades. There are six levels to the competition. Scholarships are awarded to the first place winners at the fourth, fifth, and sixth levels of the contest.

In 2013 as a freshman, Academy graduate Austin Zhang was eligible to compete in the Lions Club Student Speakers Contest for the first time. Coaching client and sophomore Alexander Danilowicz also competed in 2013. Despite it being their first year competing in this contest and being the youngest contestants, Austin and Alexander both made it all the way to the fourth level of the contest, where they competed to win a $4,500 scholarship.

In 2014 Alexander had the opportunity to compete in the fourth level of the Lions Club Student Speakers Contest again and he won the $4,500 scholarship! Alexander advanced to the fifth level of the contest, the state semi-finals, where he competed to win a $6,500 scholarship. The sixth level is the state finals contest, and the prize for winning 1st place in that contest is a $10,000 scholarship!

"Kathleen gave me practical tools, advice, and constructive critiques that gave me that extra boost of confidence to compete. Thanks to her help in molding and polishing my speech, I was able to win consistently in competitive speaking competitions. She is a real professional, and she took a big interest in my success."

Alexander Danilowicz, 11th grade, Coronado

"Kathleen helped our son with all aspects of speaking - hand gestures, voice, enunciation, facial expressions, and much more. In the end, she produced a competitive winning speaker. Our son won a $4,500 scholarship!"

Maria & Matt Danilowicz, Parents of an 11th grade student, St. Augustine

At the 2014 Del Mar Solana Beach Optimist Club Contest, graduate Austin Zhang told me aside from his parents, I am the person who has impacted his life the most. I was so touched and honored! Austin also joked he should give me a cut of his winnings. I said, "That sounds great to me!" ☺

But seriously, what a nice tribute! Austin also offered to contribute this heartfelt testimonial when he found out I was writing this book.

"The main impact you have made on me is that you opened the world of speaking to me. After taking your classes, I started to really recognize the value of speaking and I learned the difference between "speaking" and "talking." But your impact on me didn't just end there.

You have continually informed me of competition and event opportunities which my mother, and later I, learned to eagerly seize. Now I find myself a confident, competent, and proud speaker all thanks to not only the lessons I had in that hotel conference room, but also the private coaching sessions you did for me at my home before a competition and for the constant support you have given me at each and every event I have participated in.

Getting to see you again is a major motivation in my signing up for competitions, and I feel very glad to have been instructed by such an enthusiastic and funny, but still capable and strong, speaker and educator."

Austin Sun Zhang, 10th grade, Carmel Valley

Austin and Hanrui have competed in and won the Optimist Club District Level Oratorical Contest every year since they began competing. In 2011, Hanrui won 3rd place in the final level, the San Diego District Level. In 2012, Austin won 2nd place, and in 2013 Hanrui won 2nd place. In 2014, Hanrui won 1st place and the $2,500 scholarship! I'm so proud of Austin and Hanrui. I'm thankful they were inspired by my encouragement, and they accepted the challenge to compete in speech contests.

"You miss 100% of the shots you don't take."

Wayne Gretsky

"The Great One"

Former Professional Ice Hockey Player and Former Head Coach

Benefit # 10 - Ace Interviews

Private Schools, Colleges & Jobs

Another extremely essential skill is being confident enough with who you are and what you have to say so you present yourself well during interviews. Students who are shy or don't know what questions to expect are not likely to appear favorably in interviews. Being inhibited, not knowing what questions will be asked, and not rehearsing possible answers in advance can ruin your child's chances for admission to a private school or a desired college and landing his or her dream job.

Interview skills are similar to public speaking skills as they are extremely relevant to real life. However, schools do not teach this essential skill either. Thankfully, I was wise enough to take an interview skills course in college even though it was not required. I cannot imagine how awful my interviews would have been if I had not practiced what I wanted to say in advance.

At the *Academy for Public Speaking* we help students become comfortable with the interview process. By practicing their responses to the most commonly asked interview questions, students will appear confident and poised during their interviews rather than repeatedly saying "um" and "ah" as they stumble awkwardly to formulate fluent and intelligent responses.

"We are extremely happy with the confidence Kathleen has instilled in our 6th grader and the improvement in her speaking skills after just a handful of personal coaching sessions to prepare her for private school interviews. Kathleen immediately established a wonderful rapport with our daughter and worked rapidly and productively to attain maximum results with minimal time investment."

Dan & Althea Lee, Parents of a 6th grade student, Del Mar Union School District

Benefit # 11 - Embrace Leadership & Win Elections

Students at the *Academy for Public Speaking* not only increase their level of confidence and improve their public speaking skills, but they also gain valuable leadership experience. While children are at school they have become quite accustomed to the teacher being in charge, leading the class, and constantly telling them what to do and how it must be done.

At the *Academy for Public Speaking* the teacher leads the first session. However, after that the students take turns being the president and leading the meeting during each of the subsequent sessions. The president's duties begin with calling the meeting to order and sharing an inspirational message. The president also introduces the teacher, speakers, and evaluators throughout the meeting. The president presides over all aspects and adjourns the meeting at the end of the session.

In the beginning, most students are reluctant to volunteer to serve as the president. In general, they are hesitant because they have never been in charge or led a group of their peers. The students are all highly capable. However, they tend to lack confidence due to a lack of experience. The *Academy for Public Speaking* classes provide a unique opportunity for students to learn to step into and embrace the power of leadership. Students are given valuable opportunities to take responsibility, show initiative, and be assertive and decisive while also expressing their personality and creativity.

The skills students learn at the *Academy for Public Speaking* are relevant to real life. No matter which path your child decides to pursue in life, effective communication skills are essential for success. *Academy for Public Speaking* graduates apply what they have learned in other aspects of their lives, especially at school.

Graduates from our program are often inspired to pursue positions of leadership at school. For example, when *Academy for Public Speaking* graduate Chloe was in fifth grade, she became vice president at her school. The leadership skills of taking initiative, accepting responsibility, being assertive and decisive, and giving feedback effectively are essential skills your child will need if he or she wants to have the option to become a successful business owner or entrepreneur.

When nine year old Yousif Ragab was taking his level one course with the *Academy for Public Speaking*, he decided to run for school treasurer. One day after class, Yousif asked me for advice about what to say during his campaign speech. I reminded Yousif of everything he had learned about how to structure a speech and deliver a dynamic presentation. Yousif already knew what to do. He just needed a little encouragement since he was about to embark on a new experience of campaigning to become an elected official. I shared some special tips and a few words of wisdom with Yousif so he would be sure to wow his classmates.

First, Yousif shared his inspirational speech with his fourth grade class. Next, Yousif shared his amazing speech with the whole fourth grade. As his audience grew exponentially in size so did his level of confidence! Finally, Yousif spoke passionately before his entire school to share why he, Yousif Ragab, should be elected school treasurer. Yousif had discovered the power of public speaking and as a result he was proudly elected school treasurer.

Yousif's mother, Soha, told me, "The teachers still have not stopped talking about Yousif's speech and his sense of humor. He is very famous right now! Different students from other classes like to talk to him. This has made Yousif more confident, and now he shows even stronger signs of leadership.

You have been such an amazing influence on Yousif. Before your classes, he was hesitant about trying to speak in public. Yousif was too shy. Now I am so glad he has taken your classes. You helped Yousif be more confident and speak clearly to express himself and his ideas in creative ways. You have helped Yousif improve his overall level of confidence. We really appreciate it!"

Soha & Ahmed Ragab, Parents of a 4th grade student, San Diego Unified School District

It has been such a pleasure working with Yousif. His transition has been truly amazing. To see the way Yousif's eyes light up with passion, to hear the way he uses his voice emphatically with passion and sincerity, and to feel the way he commands a room is remarkable. When Yousif speaks, people take notice. They stop and listen. Yet this is what Yousif had to say because he did not always feel this way.

"When I first joined the *Academy for Public Speaking* I was scared and frightened of large crowds. I even was scared of speaking in front of one or two people. However, learning public speaking skills has changed my point of view about speaking.

Before you know it, I'm running for school treasurer and speaking in front of about 300 people. I thank Mrs. Kathleen, the Academy instructors, and all of the students for the gift of the voice because speaking is like freedom. I think joining this club was the best decision of my life."

Yousif Ragab, 4th grade, La Jolla

Benefit #12 - Experience Success

& Inspire Positive Change

The final project for our level one course is the persuasive charity speech. I created and love this project because the most important lesson we teach children at the *Academy for Public Speaking* is your voice is a powerful tool you can use to make a positive difference in the world. Sometimes we feel small, as if what we say and do doesn't matter. However, that's simply not true. What we say and do definitely matter!

For the persuasive charity speech, each child chooses a charity to represent. The students rehearse their speeches during the second to last class. The final class is not a regular class. It is a time to celebrate the students and their success! During the graduation ceremony the students showcase their public speaking skills as they present their persuasive charity speeches for family and friends.

After the speeches we individually recognize and honor each student for his or her achievements. Everyone receives a certificate and a medal engraved with his or her name, class level, and graduation date. Trophies are awarded to the 1st, 2nd, and 3rd place winners, and the 1st place winner also earns a donation for his or her charity.

During the *Academy for Public Speaking's* first three years, graduates represented and raised money for forty-one different charities. Our students have used their voices to speak passionately on behalf of non-profit organizations whose missions include improving people's lives, taking care of animals, and protecting our environment.

After graduating from the level one course and learning the basics of public speaking, your child is welcome to join the advanced class. In the advanced class students learn techniques such as using emotion, vocal variety, facial expressions, gestures, and whole body movement. Students also learn to give speeches using key word notes and no notes at all. The advanced class provides excellent opportunities for your child to become a more creative, engaging, and powerful speaker.

After graduating from the advanced course your child will have the opportunity to participate in the masters course. During the masters course students set individual goals based on a self assessment and instruction is tailored based on the students' specific goals. The students present dynamic speeches by learning to use language in different ways, including rhetorical devices such as alliteration, sounds, repetition, imagery, and symbolism.

Speeches are videotaped for the students to review at home because, along with self reflection and setting your own goals, this is one of the most powerful tools for improvement. During the masters course the students also learn debate terminology and techniques, and they participate in two debates. The masters class is an amazing course that empowers students to be self directed leaders and learners who use the most powerful tools available for improving their communication and presentation skills.

Once your child has become a confident, effective communicator, a world of opportunities will be available. Graduates are informed of opportunities to compete in speech contests, speak at festivals, and return to the *Academy for Public Speaking* as special guest speakers. Academy graduates have shared inspirational speeches at festivals throughout San Diego and Orange County, including the Spring Forward Music Festival in Escondido, the Earth Day Festival in Oceanside, and the Green Valentines Festival in Laguna Beach.

After finishing his level one course, Neil enrolled in our advanced course, and he began taking advantage of additional opportunities provided by the *Academy for Public Speaking*. Neil spoke at the Green Valentines Festival in Laguna Beach and the Earth Day Festival in Oceanside to promote the use of solar power as a solution to global climate issues. Neil also shared his experiences in a video testimonial to inspire and encourage other students to confront and overcome their fear of public speaking.

"The *Academy for Public Speaking* has taught my son effective communication skills in an encouraging and nonjudgmental environment. These classes helped my son become eloquent and self-assured. After his level one course, he became more relaxed in front of an audience and now makes compelling presentations with professionalism and aplomb. The ability to speak professionally with confidence is acquired over time so it is an advantage to begin this process at a young age."

Nandita Dhume, Parent of a 9th grade student, Poway Unified School District

Academy graduates are also invited to be special guest speakers during the free introduction to public speaking classes we offer for prospective students. The graduates introduce themselves and share how they initially felt about public speaking, what they liked about the classes, what they learned, and how our classes have helped them. The graduates also share a speech on a topic of their choice. The special guest speakers are confident role models who volunteer their time and use their voices to inspire other children to have the courage and confidence to make a choice that will significantly change the rest of their lives. I affectionately refer to the special guest speakers as members of the Academy VIP.

Academy VIP members have earned their special status by going beyond the basics. In addition to graduating from an Academy course, members of the Academy VIP have used their voices to make a positive difference in other people's lives. Graduates who have been special guest speakers for introduction classes or have recorded video testimonials have earned VIP status. This recognition is an honor graduates receive for sharing how the Academy has changed their lives and encouraging others to have the courage to confront and overcome their fear of public speaking.

Graduates who have spoken at festivals are VIP members because they have used their voices to make a positive difference in our local communities. Graduates who have competed in speech contests have also earned VIP status due to going beyond the basics, applying their public speaking skills, and sharing their inspiration with others.

One outstanding special graduate, Priya Garcia, has frequently volunteered her time to assist with numerous classes and graduation ceremonies. Priya is a member of the original *Academy for Public Speaking* class, and during the summer of 2013 she became the *Academy for Public Speaking's* first intern.

"The Academy opened many doors for me. I learned how to organize my thoughts into words, communicate those words to an audience, and acquire a bit of money for college when the occasional panel of judges enjoyed my speech. When Kathleen asks me for help with anything, how can I refuse to carry on the Academy's great work by being a guest speaker and even an intern? I hope the Academy does as much for you as it has for me."

Priya Garcia, 12th grade, Carmel Valley

"Kathleen Petrone is a teacher who is calm, non-intimidating, and above all extremely committed to her students. My daughters have taken her level one and advanced public speaking classes. This has inspired them to join the speech and debate team at their high school as well as enter speech contests in the community.

Kathleen not only informs my daughters about contests, but she also comes to watch them compete. Kathleen has attended their speech and debate events and has even been a volunteer judge. Kathleen even came to see my daughter in her high school play! That is true dedication! It takes a village to raise a child--I'm lucky to have Kathleen in my village!"

Bhuvana Ramanathan, Parent of 9th & 12th grade students, San Dieguito Union High School District

A very special group of Academy VIP members volunteered to participate in a photo shoot for the cover of this book and the *Academy for Public Speaking* brochure. Seeing the graduates' confident, happy faces warms my heart and fills me with pride because they remind me of the mission of the *Academy for Public Speaking*. We inspire and empower children to become confident, effective communicators. However, the power of public speaking will not only positively impact your child's life. Your child will also inspire other people and make a positive difference in their lives as well.

The transformation from painful to powerful truly is amazing. By embracing the power of public speaking we can teach confidence, touch hearts, and transform lives. Confidence is the key to success and happiness.

"Too many of us are not living our dreams because we are living our fears."

Les Brown

Motivational Speaker, Trainer & Bestselling Author

National Television & Radio Talk Show Host

Epilogue

Unleashing my fear and unlocking the power of public speaking...

Deciding to confront and conquer my fear of public speaking felt like a monumental, scary decision at the time. Yet, thankfully, my intuition was insistently telling me it was time to make a change. And, thankfully, I listened to that inner voice and accepted the challenge.

Deciding to confront and conquer my fear of public speaking has positively impacted my life in numerous ways, both personally and professionally. Through my involvement with Toastmasters, I gained the confidence and communication skills to feel comfortable expressing my ideas and desires. Feeling confident enough to share my emotions with my husband, Russ Petrone, played a significant role in convincing him I was Mrs. Right.

Having the confidence to creatively express myself in front of others, especially at Toastmasters meetings and events, has earned me the enjoyment of new, high quality friendships. With only three days notice, I emailed Jimmy, Jim, Norm, Mila, and Surraju to say I would feel honored if they would contribute a testimonial to this book. With such short notice, I would have understood if anyone didn't have the time. Yet every one of my friends I asked took the time to contribute their thoughts. A 100% response rate – nice!

As a result of embracing the power of public speaking, my behavior has improved too! Being willing to go through the "awkward stage" allowed me to make the transition from painful to powerful. Before joining Toastmasters, I avoided responsibility and taking initiative. I was indecisive and unassertive. Can you imagine becoming a successful entrepreneur or business owner with these qualities?

These traits were not serving me well in my personal or professional life. By developing my communication and leadership skills, I successfully reversed these negative traits. While building my confidence and communication skills, I also had the good fortune to discover my passion and purpose in life – teaching children confidence, public speaking, and leadership skills. Prior to discovering my passion and purpose, I was a classroom teacher for eleven years. However, teaching the state standards was not nearly as exciting or rewarding as teaching children confidence and effective communication skills!

By facing my fear, I have been handsomely rewarded. I live a life I truly love. As an entrepreneur and a business owner, I have greater liberty in my life than when I taught for public and private schools. I met the man of my dreams, and I married him. I freely express my thoughts, and I no longer live in fear of being afraid to speak, make a mistake, or take a risk I know is right for me.

But the true beauty is now I have earned the honor and privilege of helping children realize, at a much younger age than I did, that confidence is the key to happiness and success.

I've learned it's generally a good idea to avoid, "What if...?" questions. But what if I had not faced my fear of public speaking? Would I be a successful entrepreneur? Would I be happily married? Would I have discovered my passion and purpose in life? Would I have positively impacted hundreds and then thousands of children's lives?

No, sadly, the Academy for Public Speaking would not exist because I would not have joined Toastmasters. That is where I gained my confidence and courage. That is where I discovered my passion and purpose. That is where and when I decided despite lacking a background in business, I not only could, but I would become a successful entrepreneur!

Maybe I would have been lucky enough to still marry Russ. It's hard to say. But what I know for certain is confidence is the key to your child's success. Give your child the gift that lasts a lifetime – the gift of confidence! ☺

Acknowledgements

Special thanks to my amazing husband, Russ Petrone, who introduced me to a path I did not even know existed, where I discovered the power of personal growth. Exploring personal growth led me down the path to finding and fulfilling my soul purpose in life, which has consequently led to continued happiness and success. Russ, I am truly grateful for your kind and generous spirit, which has touched more lives than you know. Your love and support have not only allowed me to flourish, but have also lovingly contributed to the creation, development, and expansion of the *Academy for Public Speaking*. You inspired me to step outside my comfort zone, take emotional and financial risks, and have continually encouraged my entrepreneurial spirit. On behalf of all the lives of the Academy students you have already positively impacted and will impact in the future, as well as mine, thank you for touching our hearts and making our world a better place. I love you! ☺

Special thanks to my fabulous mother, Julie Behrens, who is not only a wonderful mother, but also a seriously dedicated editor and a source of advice and wisdom! I feel truly blessed to have enjoyed such a happy, positive childhood as part of a loving family. Special thanks to my father, Ralph Behrens, and my sister, Teresa Schmitter, for being part of our happy family and supporting me in everything I do. And a special shout out to my bro, mid-Mo Joe, and my nieces Gretchen and Kyra. Girls, keep pestering your parents about when you will get to come to California to see Aunt Kat! Persistence is a virtue. ☺

Special thanks to Linda Clark for the conversation we had in the parking lot of the Carmel Valley Rec Center in 2010. That was the magical day when the proverbial light bulb clicked on, and I discovered my passion and purpose in life. To my SCORE mentors, Pat Stewart and Dennis Ferguson, thank you for sharing your wisdom and guidance. There is no greater joy than living my passion and purpose!

Special thanks to my friends Jimmy Thai, Jim Tucker, Norm Nomura, Julie Geisbauer, Surraju Nadimpalli, and Mila Diamond for your contributions. One of the greatest rewards of joining Toastmasters has been meeting friends of your caliber. Each one of you touches so many lives in so many ways, especially mine. Thank you for inspiring my students and me by sharing your wisdom and talent during your visits as special guest speakers. Thank you to my dear friends Judge Rose Waring and Editor Extraordinaire John Stark. Johnny Garon, thanks for calling me chicken. Bawk!

Special thanks to Natalya Abramovich, Andrea Sun, Judith Blue, Ahmed & Soha Ragab, Zach Hornby, Dan & Althea Lee, Meiling Yueh, Yu Sun, Bhuvana Ramanathan, Maria & Matt Danilowicz, & Nandita Dhume for your testimonials!

A very special thanks to the members of the Academy VIP - Priya Garcia, Solana Garcia, Chloe Stevenson, Hanrui Zhang, Austin Zhang, Neil Majumdar, Kelly Hu, Sachel Jetly, Alexander Danilowicz, Daniel Kalotov, Yousif Ragab, Megan Corrigan, Sydney Corrigan, Andrew Zhou, James Huang, Pranathi Rao, Sudeepti Rao, Toren Dunbar, Elle Laikind, Miles Blue, Lilia Arami, and all other contestants and special guest speakers!

Special thanks to John Surge for creating the gorgeous *Academy for Public Speaking* marketing materials, including the cover for this book. John, thanks for your patience with my analytic mind and perfectionistic tendencies. Thank you also for prioritizing this project on the weekend of the Masters Golf Tournament. Your excellence, effort, and dedication are exceptional! Thanks to photographers Leslie Bird, Payton Beckman, De Martin, and Patrick Lockwood for capturing such beautiful shots and making John's job so easy. Ha, ha. Just kidding, John.

Special thanks to Meiling Yueh and Willie Nelson for being the biggest *Academy for Public Speaking* Facebook fans! We love you too! ☺ Linda Luetje Nelson, love you too!

And last, but certainly not least, thank you to every *Academy for Public Speaking* graduate for having the courage to become a confident, effective communicator and using your voice to inspire others and make our world a better place. I wish you a lifetime of success & happiness!

Sincerely,

Kathleen

Distinguished Toastmaster Kathleen Petrone is the president and founder of the *Academy for Public Speaking*, a credentialed educator, and a highly successful speech coach. With a Master's Degree in education and over 15 years of experience, this dynamic, award-winning speaker creatively inspires and empowers children to become confident, effective communicators.

Academy for Public Speaking graduates win top honors and cash prizes in annual speech contests held by the Lions Club, the Optimist Club, the North South Foundation, and the San Diego County Fair Board. In 2014 graduate Hanrui Zhang won a $2,500 scholarship and coaching client Alexander Danilowicz won a $4,500 scholarship!

Most importantly, graduates of the *Academy for Public Speaking* learn their voices are powerful tools they can use to make a positive difference in our world.

Kathleen is also a contributing author to the books *Next Level Speaking* by Excelsior Toastmasters and *Imagine Wisdom Education*. To contact Kathleen, please visit…

www.AcademyForPublicSpeaking.com

"If you're not brave enough to take the first step, then you'll never know how far you can go."

Nishan Panwar

Made in the USA
Middletown, DE
26 October 2016